POCAHONTAS
and the
POWHATANS

By Reese Donaghey

Gareth Stevens
PUBLISHING

Please visit our website, www.garethstevens.com. For a free color catalog of all our high-quality books, call toll free 1-800-542-2595 or fax 1-877-542-2596.

Library of Congress Cataloging-in-Publication Data

Connors, Kathleen.
 Pocahontas and the Powhatans / Kathleen Connors.
    pages cm. — (What you didn't know about history)
 Includes index.
ISBN 978-1-4824-1938-2 (pbk.)
ISBN 978-1-4824-1937-5 (6 pack)
ISBN 978-1-4824-1939-9 (library binding)
1. Pocahontas, -1617—Juvenile literature. 2. Powhatan women—Biography—Juvenile
literature. 3. Smith, John, 1580-1631—Juvenile literature. 4. Virginia—History—Colonial
period, ca. 1600-1775—Juvenile literature. I. Title.
E99.P85C66 2015
975.5'01092—dc23
 [B]
                                                    2014026088

First Edition

Published in 2015 by
Gareth Stevens Publishing
111 East 14th Street, Suite 349
New York, NY 10003

Designer: Andrea Davison-Bartolotta
Editor: Kristen Rajczak

Photo credits: Cover, pp. 1, 19 Kean Collection/Getty Images; p. 5 Peter Dennis/Getty Images; p. 7 (inset) Daniella Nowitz/National Geographic/Getty Images; p. 7 (main) Marilyn Angel Wynn/Nativestock/Getty Images; p. 8 Tim Graham/Getty Images; p. 9 DEA/G. Dagli Orti/De Agostini Picture Library/Getty Images; p. 10 Nikater/Wikimedia Commons; p. 11 Hulton Archive/Getty Images; p. 13 SuperStock/Getty Images; p. 15 MPI/ Getty Images; p. 17 Three Lions/Getty Images; p. 20 Visions of America/UIG/Getty Images.

Printed in the United States of America

CPSIA compliance information: Batch #CW15GS: For further information contact Gareth Stevens, New York, New York at 1-800-542-2595.

CONTENTS

Words in the glossary appear in **bold** type the first time they are used in the text.

BEHIND THE STORIES

Pocahontas was the daughter of the great Powhatan chief Wahunsonacock (wah-huhn-SEHN-uh-kawh). Historians aren't certain about much of her life. Everything known about her was either written by English settlers or is part of Native American **oral history** hundreds of years old—and these stories don't agree!

Nonetheless, much of her daily life can be based on what is known about Powhatan communities during the early 1600s. Even though she was Wahunsonacock's daughter, she would have lived similarly to other Powhatan girls.

Did You Know?

Pocahontas was born around 1596 and named Amonute, though she was sometimes called Matoaka. "Pocahontas" was a nickname that meant "playful one."

The English settlers called Wahunsonacock "Chief Powhatan." He came from a village called Powhatan, and the group of Native American tribes he brought together under his power also became known by that name.

*I*N THE VILLAGE

The Powhatans mostly lived in villages around the waterways of present-day Virginia. Each settlement had two to 100 houses with six to 20 people living in each. The homes were called *yehakins* and were built by the women of the village. Women also raised the Powhatan children.

Growing up as a Powhatan child, Pocahontas wouldn't have been wearing much! Until she was a young teenager, Pocahontas also would have had most of her head shaved except one long piece in the back.

Did You Know?

At the time Pocahontas lived, her father was top chief of more than 30 tribes with a total population of about 25,000. Each tribe had its own lesser chief, too.

Yehakins *were made of saplings, or young trees, bent into a rounded shape and tied together. Mats were woven and placed over the saplings.*

inside a yehakin

WOMEN WORK, MEN MAKE WAR

Powhatan women did the farming and cooking in their villages. They found firewood and made baskets, pots, and clothing. They often **tattooed** their bodies with pictures and shapes.

Powhatan men hunted, fished for food, and went to war as needed. They had a haircut suited to these jobs. Half of a Powhatan man's head was shaved so his **bowstring** wouldn't get caught in his hair! The women used **mussel** shells to shave the men's heads. Their heads weren't usually very smooth!

8

Did You Know?
Both men and women painted their face and body for special occasions. The colors they used depended on the occasion!

Boys and girls learned the **traditional** men's and women's jobs as they grew up. Pocahontas had to learn to work like all Powhatan women, even as the chief's daughter.

9

ENTER THE ENGLISH

In 1607, the English built their first lasting settlement in North America at Jamestown. It was right in Powhatan territory! Pocahontas was around 11 years old when her people first met the English settlers.

One of the settlers is still famous today—John Smith. Very soon after arriving at Jamestown, Smith set out to explore the land around Jamestown. He would go on to write a lot about it and the Powhatans he met while mapping and studying the land.

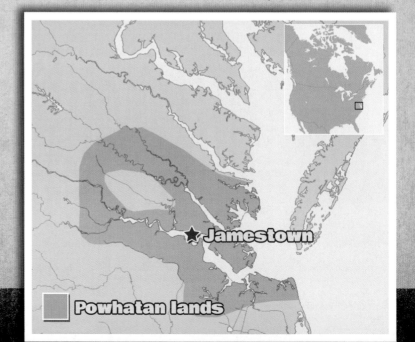

Powhatan lands

Native Americans had been living in present-day Virginia for about 12,000 years. The building of Jamestown wouldn't be the last time their land was taken by settlers.

Did You Know?

Smith was captured by Powhatan's brother Opechancanough while out exploring in 1607.

TWO STORIES

Most people think they know the story of John Smith and Pocahontas. What they know is Smith's account of the story. In it, Smith wrote that Powhatan was about to kill him when Pocahontas jumped in the way. Historians say his life probably wasn't in danger at all!

Furthermore, according to the oral history of a Powhatan tribe called the Mattaponi, Pocahontas likely wasn't even there. It was probably a **ceremony** that may have been **religious**. Children wouldn't have been allowed to attend.

Did You Know?

John Smith wrote that Pocahontas saved his life *again* a few years later. The Mattaponi history says that's probably untrue, too.

GIFTS AND GREED

Historical accounts do agree that Pocahontas met John Smith. She would have known him from her visits to Jamestown. Powhatan gave food and supplies to the settlers who were not yet growing their own food well. Pocahontas accompanied these gifts as a sign of peace.

However, a terrible **drought** reduced the Powhatans' harvests. By the winter of 1608 to 1609, they had less to give the settlers. Powhatan decided his tribes would no longer supply the English for another reason, too: He felt they'd gotten **greedy**.

The winter of 1609 to 1610 was called the "starving time." Neither Powhatans nor Jamestown settlers had enough to eat then.

Did You Know?

The Powhatans spoke one of a group of related native languages called Algonquian, not English. In order to overcome the language **barrier**, a few English and Powhatan boys were chosen to live with and learn the ways and words of their new neighbors.

OF MARRYING AGE

Pocahontas would have been considered ready for marriage in the Powhatan **culture** around age 14. It was around this time when the connection between her people and the settlers was beginning to be quite unfriendly.

Most Powhatans were allowed to choose whom they'd marry. Powhatan men had to win over a woman's parents, first. That means Kocoum, the man Pocahontas chose to marry, had to ask the most powerful man in the tribe for permission! She was about 14 years old when they married.

Did You Know?

Powhatan men paid a "bride wealth" to the family of the woman they wanted to marry. It was payment for the loss of their daughter.

A Powhatan man would bring a woman's parents food to show he could take care of their daughter and any children they might have.

TAKEN PRISONER

In 1613, the English kidnapped Pocahontas! Captain Samuel Argell was unhappy that the Powhatans still weren't trading with the settlers. He thought he could use Pocahontas to make her father change his mind.

There are two stories about what happened next. According to English history, Pocahontas learned to speak English and fell in love with a wealthy man named John Rolfe. The Mattaponi say Rolfe forced Pocahontas into a **relationship**. This account also says Captain Argell had Kocoum killed.

Did You Know?

In 1614, Pocahontas changed her name to Rebecca. She also started to follow the Christian religion of the English.

Rolfe married Pocahontas in April 1614. Her father agreed to the marriage, but some say he worried what would happen to his daughter if he didn't.

POCAHONTAS AND BEYOND

Pocahontas, Rolfe, and their son went to England in 1616. Pocahontas's sister and a few other Powhatans went with them. They were planning to draw new settlers to Virginia. Then, in March 1617, Pocahontas suddenly got sick on the ship getting ready to return to Jamestown. She died quickly and is buried in the English town of Gravesend.

Pocahontas's people live on today. There are seven recognized Powhatan tribes in Virginia, including the Upper Mattaponi, with a total population of about 3,400.

modern-day Powhatans

Did You Know?
The Powhatans in England with Pocahontas, including her sister, thought she had been poisoned.

True or False?

Stories about Pocahontas don't always match up with history!

Pocahontas was the daughter of the great chief Powhatan.

True, but she was born with the name Amonute, not Pocahontas.

Pocahontas saved John Smith's life.

False. It's unlikely he was in danger and also unlikely she was there. He may have made up the story!

Pocahontas knew John Smith.

True, but she was only a child when she knew him, and he left Virginia not long after in 1609.

Pocahontas fell in love with John Rolfe and wanted to marry him.

English accounts say **true**. Powhatan oral history says **false**.

GLOSSARY

barrier: something that makes progress hard

bowstring: the string joining the ends of a shooting bow, which is a curved tool used with arrows for hunting and fighting

ceremony: an event to honor or celebrate something

culture: the beliefs and ways of life of a group of people

drought: a long period of very dry weather

greedy: having a strong wish for more goods than needed

mussel: a small freshwater animal with a shell

oral history: accounts passed down by word of mouth

relationship: a connection to another person, including one of love

religious: having to do with a belief in and way of honoring a god or gods

tattoo: to mark with tattoos, or permanent markings on the skin

traditional: having to do with long-practiced customs

FOR MORE INFORMATION

Books

Fay, Gail. *Pocahontas.* Chicago, IL: Heinemann Library, 2013.

King, David C. *The Powhatan.* New York, NY: Marshall Cavendish Benchmark, 2008.

Websites

Famous Native Americans
mrnussbaum.com/famous
Learn about the lives of several Native Americans, such as Sitting Bull and Tecumseh.

Powhatan Indian Fact Sheet
www.bigorrin.org/powhatan_kids.htm
Read much more about the Powhatan tribe.

INDEX